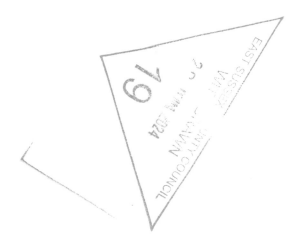

Continents
Infographics

By Harriet Brundle

Designed by Charlotte Neve

©2017
Book Life
King's Lynn
Norfolk PE30 4LS

ISBN: 978-1-78637-204-8

Written by:
Harriet Brundle

Edited by:
Charlie Ogden

Designed by:
Charlotte Neve

A catalogue record
for this book is
available from
the British Library.

BookLife
Publishing
.com

Continents
Infographics

Contents

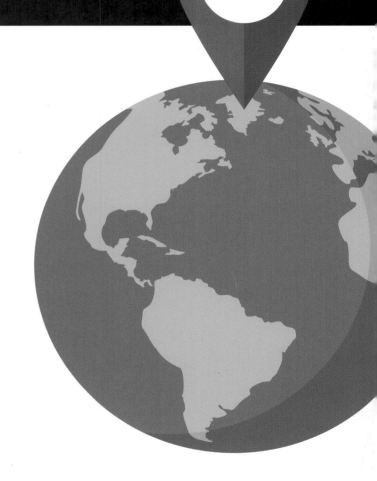

Words that are <u>underlined</u> are explained in the glossary on page 31.

The Seven Continents

It is estimated that our planet is around **4,543,000,000** years old.

A continent is a very large <u>landmass</u> that is usually made up of lots of different countries. In total, there are seven different continents on planet Earth.

Europe

Asia

North America

Africa

South America

Australia

Antarctica

There are over **7,000,000,000** people living in the world and every single one of them lives on one of the Earth's seven continents.

The continents are separated by five large oceans and several smaller oceans and seas.

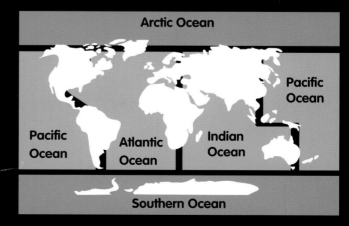

Arctic Ocean

Pacific Ocean

Pacific Ocean

Atlantic Ocean

Indian Ocean

Southern Ocean

3,800,000,000 years ago, water appeared on the <u>surface</u> of the planet. Now, over **70%** of the Earth's surface is covered in water.

Africa

Madagascar

islands are usually said to be a part of their nearest continent.

The island of Madagascar is part of Africa.

The continents, as well as the countries that make them up, are split into time zones. A time zone is a region where the same time is used by everyone. When you travel to a different country on holiday, you may move into a different time zone.

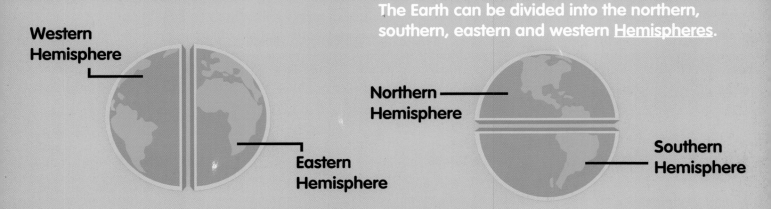

United States of America

United Kingdom

China

London

New York

Hong Kong

The Earth can be divided into the northern, southern, eastern and western Hemispheres.

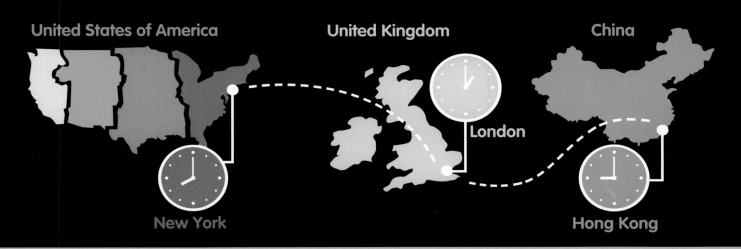

Western Hemisphere

Eastern Hemisphere

Northern Hemisphere

Southern Hemisphere

Imagine the Earth has been split into one large grid and each line on the grid has been given a number. At points where two lines meet, the number from each of the lines is given to that point. These numbers are known as the coordinates of that place. Every place on Earth has a coordinate. These numbers act like an address that anyone on the planet can understand, no matter what language they speak.

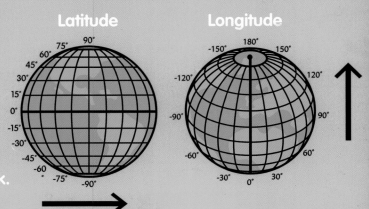

Latitude

Longitude

Asia

Asia is the largest continent on Earth. It covers almost **9%** of Earth's surface and makes up **30%** of the land on Earth.

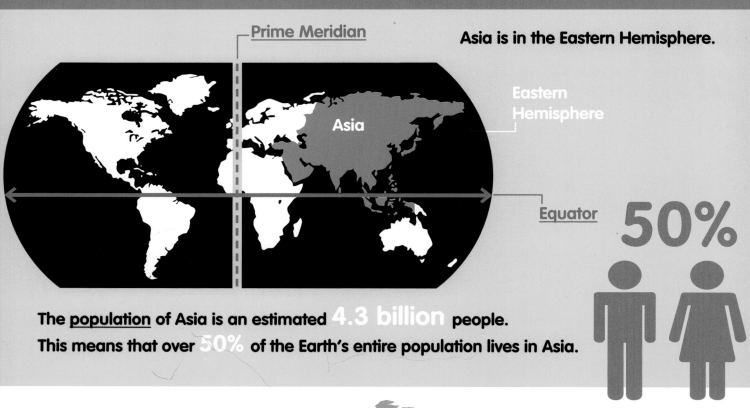

Prime Meridian

Asia is in the Eastern Hemisphere.

Asia

Eastern Hemisphere

Equator

50%

The <u>population</u> of Asia is an estimated **4.3 billion** people.
This means that over **50%** of the Earth's entire population lives in Asia.

RUSSIA

KAZAKHSTAN

MONGOLIA

UZBEKISTAN

TURKEY

TURKMENISTAN

KYRGYZSTAN

NORTH KOREA

SOUTH KOREA

JAPAN

SYRIA

IRAQ

IRAN

AFGHANISTAN

CHINA

PAKISTAN

SAUDI ARABIA

INDIA

OMAN

BURMA

YEMEN

THAILAND

CAMBODIA

PHILIPPINES

SRI LANKA

MALAYSIA

INDONESIA

Countries in Asia include China, Japan and India.

China is the most populated country in the world. It is one of only two countries to have a population of **over 1,000,000,000.**

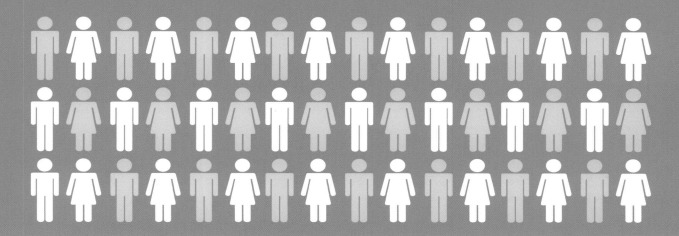

The largest country in Asia is Russia. Russia is also the biggest country in the world – it is so big that it even stretches into Europe.

Asia has the longest coastline of all the continents, measuring in at about 62,800 km in length.

Some countries in Asia are extremely busy and highly populated. Other countries, such as Mongolia, have large expanses of land that are <u>uninhabited</u>.

Saudi Arabia, a country in Asia, is home to one of the largest sandy <u>deserts</u> in the world. It is known as the Arabian Desert.

Mount Everest, the tallest mountain in the world, is in Asia. It lies directly on the <u>border</u> between Nepal and China. It rises over 8,800 metres above sea level.

8,800 m

Africa

Africa is the second largest continent in the world.

There are parts of Africa in all four hemispheres.

NORTH AFRICA

MOROCCO
ALGERIA
LIBYA
EGYPT
WESTERN SAHARA
MAURITANIA
MALI
NIGER
CHAD
SUDAN
SOMALIA
ETHIOPIA
SENEGAL
GUINEA
NIGERIA
SOUTH SUDAN
SIERRA LEONE
IVORY COAST
GHANA
CENTRAL AFRICAN REPUBLIC
CAMEROON

WEST AFRICA

EQUATORIAL GUINEA
UGANDA
KENYA

CENTRAL AFRICA

GABON
DEMONCRATIC REPUBLIC OF THE CONGO
TANZANIA

EAST AFRICA

REPUBLIC OF THE CONGO

Africa is home to 15% of the world's population – that's over 1,000,000,000 people. It is the second most populated continent.

ANGOLA
ZAMBIA
MALAWI
ZIMBABWE
MOZAMBIQUE
NAMIBIA
BOTSWANA
MADAGASCAR
SWAZILAND
SOUTH AFRICA

The continent is often divided into five regions – north, south, east, west and central Africa. Within these regions, there are 54 different countries.

SOUTH AFRICA

The Equator runs through the centre of Africa. In total, the Equator passes through six different countries in Africa.

The prime meridian also runs through Africa.

Africa is the hottest continent on Earth.

The northern part of Africa is mostly dry grasslands and deserts, while the southern part of the continent has dense rainforests and <u>savannahs</u>.

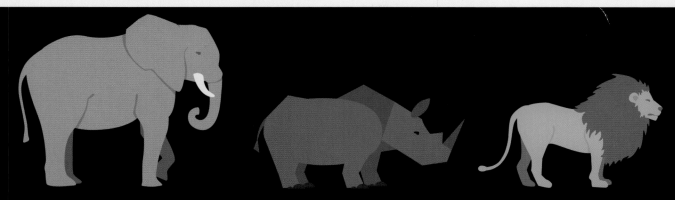

Africa is home to lots of <u>endangered</u> animals, including the African elephant, the black rhinoceros and the African lion.

One of the longest rivers in the world, the Nile, is found in Africa. It flows through several different countries, including Uganda, Ethiopia and Egypt.

Egypt

River Nile

Sudan

Ethiopia

South
Sudan

**40,000,000
people**

The largest country in Africa is Algeria. It has a population of over 40,000,000.

Uganda

Antarctica

Antarctica is the farthest south of all the continents. It is home to the South Pole, which is the most southern point on the surface of the Earth. It is on the opposite side of the Earth to the North Pole.

The Antarctic region, which is known as the Antarctic Circle, is the southernmost of the five major circles of latitude on Earth.

North Pole

South Pole

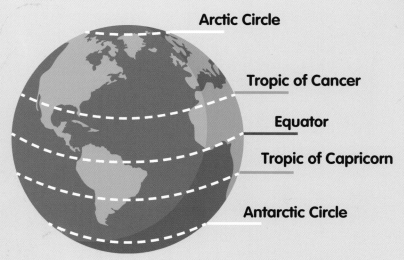

Arctic Circle

Tropic of Cancer

Equator

Tropic of Capricorn

Antarctic Circle

-89.2°C

Antarctica is the **coldest** and **windiest** continent. The coldest temperature ever recorded on Earth was -89.2°C. It was recorded at Vostok Station in Antarctica. The surface of Antarctica is made up of large glaciers.

Around **98%** of Antarctica is covered in ice. The majority of the fresh water in the world is held in the ice in Antarctica.

COLD

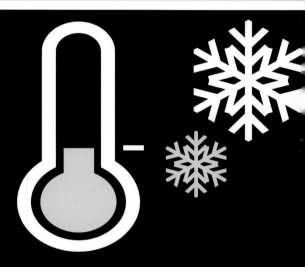

There are no cities or villages in Antarctica. The weather is so extreme that it is uninhabitable for humans, which is why it is the least populated continent on Earth.

There are no individual countries in Antarctica.

Animals such as penguins, seals and albatrosses can be found in Antarctica at certain times of the year. However, most animals do not live there all year round as the weather in winter is too cold for them to survive.

Antarctica is nearly twice the size of Australia and it is the **fifth largest** continent on Earth.

Australia

Australia is a country in the Southern Hemisphere. However, Australia is also the name of the continent the country is a part of. The Australian continent is home to many other countries as well as Australia, including New Zealand, Papua New Guinea and Fiji.

Australia is the sixth largest country in the world and is over 7,600,000 km² in size.

Southern Hemisphere

Australia

Australia has a population of over 24,000,000 people.

Some of the largest cities in Australia include Sydney, Melbourne, Brisbane, Perth and Adelaide.

Northern Territory

Western Australia

Perth

Queensland

Brisbane

South Australia

New South Wales

Adelaide

Sydney

Melbourne

Victoria

Tasmania

Australia has a range of different landscapes, including rainforests, mountains and deserts.

The capital city of Australia is called Canberra.

Over **60%** of the country is covered by desert and is often referred to as the Australian Outback. This area is largely uninhabited.

2,228 Metres

One of the highest mountains in Australia is called Mount Kosciuszko. It is 2,228 metres high.

Eastern Brown Snake

Sydney Funnel-Web Spider

Australia is well known for having some of the world's most dangerous animals, including poisonous spiders and snakes.

Ayers Rock, found in Australia, is the largest standing rock in the world. The rock is thought to be around

600 million years old.

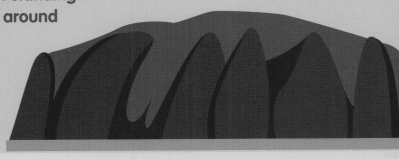

Australia is home to the largest <u>coral reef</u> in the world, called the Great Barrier Reef. Scientists believe that there are over **1,500** different <u>species</u> of fish living in the reef.

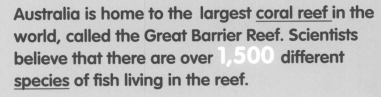

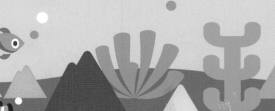

Europe

Europe is the second **smallest** continent on Earth. Countries in Europe include England, Italy, Germany, Greece and Sweden.

The population of Europe is over **738 million**. Although Europe is small in size, it has the third largest population of any continent.

Europe covers **2%** of the Earth's surface.

Russia

Europe

Asia

Sweden

England

Germany

Italy

Greece

The country Russia spans across both Europe and Asia. The part of Russia that is in Europe covers around **40%** of Europe's total land area.

Europe has a range of different landscapes including beaches, rivers, mountains and forests.

The longest beach in Europe is in **France.**
The beach, called La Baule-Escoublac, is 12 km long.

12 km

Europe — Eastern Hemisphere

Europe is part of a giant landmass that consists of Europe and Asia.

This landmass is called **Eurasia.** Europe makes up the western part of the Eurasian landmass.

Asia

Europe

Europe is mostly in the Eastern Hemisphere, although part of it is found in the Western Hemisphere.

Europe is home to the smallest country in the world – Vatican City. Vatican City has a population of just 1000 people. It is around eight times smaller than New York's Central Park.

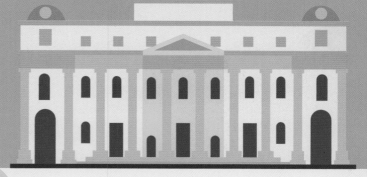

The largest mountain range in Europe is called the Alps. The tallest mountain in the Alps is Mont Blanc.

Mont Blanc is over 4.8 km tall!

15

North America

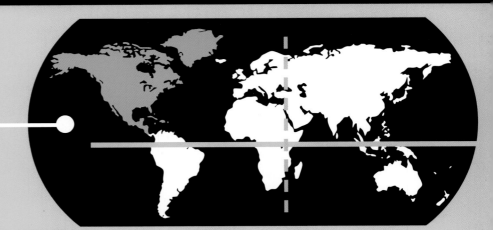

North America lies entirely in the Northern Hemisphere. It is the third largest continent in the world.

There are a total of **23 countries** in North America. The majority of the land is taken up by Canada, the United States of America and Mexico. Other countries in North America include Panama and Jamaica.

CANADA

UNITED STATES OF AMERICA

MEXICO

Jamaica

Panama

Over 565 million

The population of North America is over 565 million. The country in North America with the highest population is the U.S.A.

The world's largest fresh water lake, called Lake Superior, is found in North America. It measures an estimated 82,103 km². That's roughly the same size as the country of Austria!

ONTARIO

82,103 km²

MINNESOTA

MICHIGAN

Mexico experiences a lot of earthquakes. One of the strongest earthquakes to hit Mexico measured in at an 8.1 on the Richter scale.

Death Valley in the U.S.A. is one of the hottest places on Earth. It is also the lowest point on the North American continent.

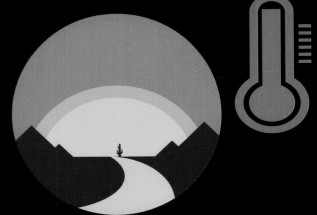

The landscape in North America includes deserts, taigas and grasslands.

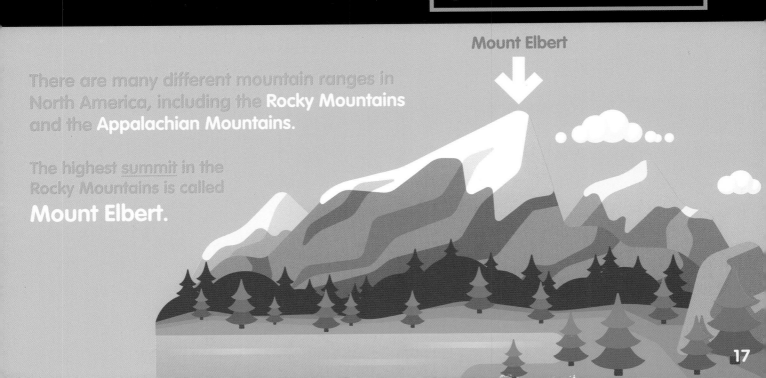

Mount Elbert

There are many different mountain ranges in North America, including the **Rocky Mountains** and the **Appalachian Mountains**.

The highest summit in the Rocky Mountains is called **Mount Elbert.**

South America

- **ECUADOR**
- **PERU**
- **BRAZIL**
- **CHILE**
- **ARGENTINA**

South America is the fourth largest continent. It has a population of over 422 million people.

There are **12** countries in South America, including Brazil, Argentina, Peru, Ecuador and Chile.

Brazil is the largest country in South America and it covers almost half of the continent's landmass. São Paulo, a city in Brazil, is the largest city in South America and the 12th largest city in the world.

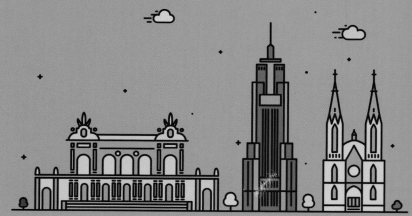

Almost all of South America lies in the Southern Hemisphere, with only a small part breaking into the Northern Hemisphere.

The Amazon River in South America is one of the longest rivers in the world. There are thousands of different species of fish living in the Amazon.

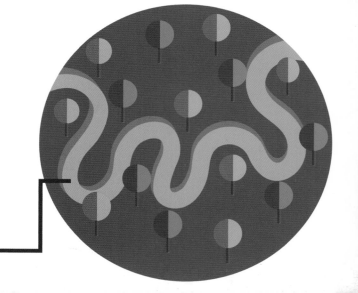

The landscapes in South America vary hugely.

The Atacama Desert in Chile is one of the driest places on Earth.

The Andes mountain range in South America is the longest above-ground mountain range in the world.

A large portion of South America is covered by rainforests. The largest of these rainforests is the Amazon rainforest, which is spread across nine different countries.

Suriname is the smallest country in South America. The official language of Suriname is Dutch.

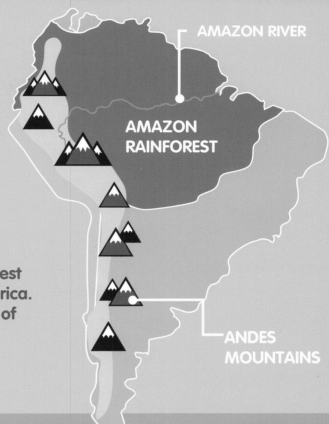

AMAZON RIVER

AMAZON RAINFOREST

ANDES MOUNTAINS

Angel Falls in Venezuela is the highest waterfall in the world. It is nearly **1000 metres tall.**

Piranha fish

Caiman

South America is home to animals such as jaguars, piranha fish and caiman.

19

The Five Oceans

Our Earth is made up of large landmasses, called continents, and large bodies of water, called oceans.

Find out more about this on page 26.

Millions of years ago, all the land on Earth was in one huge landmass that was surrounded by water. This single landmass is known today as Pangea. Over time, Pangea split up into pieces and began to spread out through the ocean. Although the water on Earth is all connected, it is often broken up into five separate oceans.

Pangea

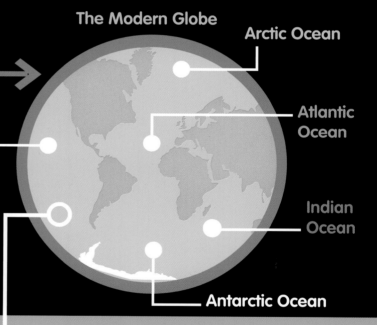

The Modern Globe

Arctic Ocean

Pacific Ocean

Atlantic Ocean

Indian Ocean

Antarctic Ocean

The five oceans are called:
1. Pacific Ocean
2. Atlantic Ocean
3. Indian Ocean
4. Arctic Ocean
5. Antarctic Ocean

The Pacific Ocean is the largest ocean in the world, covering over **165,000,000 km²**.

Over 97% of the water on Earth is the salt water found in our oceans.

The Pacific Ocean alone covers around **30%** of the Earth's surface!

The Pacific Ocean is split into the **North** and **South Pacific.**

The continents of Asia, Australia, South America and North America all touch the Pacific Ocean.

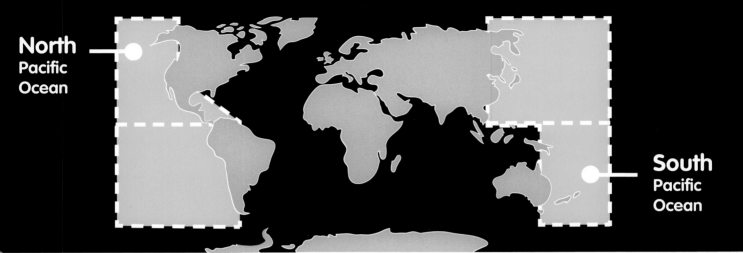

North
Pacific
Ocean

South
Pacific
Ocean

While its name means 'peaceful sea', the Pacific Ocean is far from calm. It is actually home to the 'Ring of Fire'.

This is a ring of volcanoes that regularly erupt. This area also regularly experiences earthquakes.

Challenger Deep

Pacific Ocean

Ring of Fire

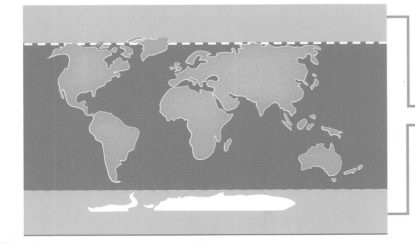

The deepest point in the Earth's oceans is found in the Pacific Ocean. It is known as the Challenger Deep and it is part of the Mariana Trench.

The Arctic Ocean lies to the north of the Pacific Ocean and the Antarctic Ocean lies to the south of the Pacific Ocean.

The Five Oceans

The Atlantic Ocean is the second biggest ocean in the world.

The Equator runs through the Atlantic Ocean, dividing it into the North Atlantic Ocean and the South Atlantic Ocean.

The Atlantic Ocean covers around **20%** of the Earth's surface.

The Atlantic Ocean touches North America, South America, Europe and Africa.

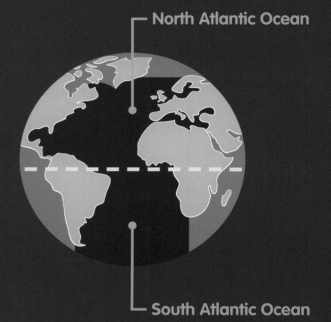

North Atlantic Ocean

South Atlantic Ocean

Animals living in the Atlantic Ocean include whales, dolphins, turtles and seals.

The Atlantic Ocean is home to the second largest coral reef in the world. It is called the **Great Mayan Reef** and it lies off the coast of Mexico, Guatemala and Belize.

The Atlantic Ocean is roughly **6.5** times the size of the U.S.A.

The Indian Ocean is the third largest ocean in the world.

Australia, Asia and Africa all touch the Indian Ocean.

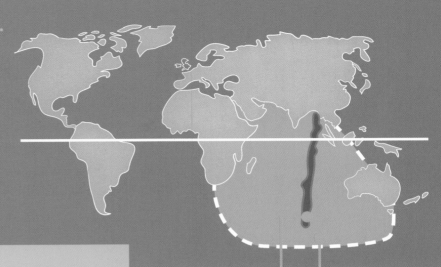

Indian Ocean

Ninety East Ridge

5,000 km

An underwater mountain range called the Ninety East Ridge divides the Indian Ocean into East and West regions. It is around 5,000 km in length.

The deepest part of the Indian Ocean is called the Sunda Trench. It is over **7.7 km** deep.

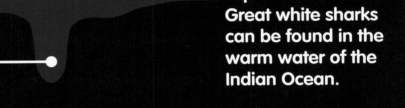

Sunda Trench

Great white sharks can be found in the warm water of the Indian Ocean.

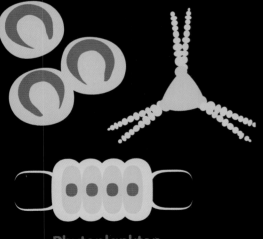

Phytoplankton

The Indian Ocean is the warmest of all Earth's oceans. The warm temperature makes it more difficult for sea life to survive. This is because <u>phytoplankton</u> cannot grow as well in warm temperatures. Lots of different species of animal in the ocean rely on phytoplankton as a food source.

The Indian Ocean is rich in <u>oil</u>. It is thought that around 40% of the world's offshore oil comes from this ocean.

The Five Oceans

The Arctic Ocean is the smallest and shallowest of all the oceans.

The Arctic Ocean is located around the North Pole and it touches the continents of Europe, Asia and North America.

The Arctic Ocean is almost entirely landlocked, as it is surrounded by Greenland, Alaska, Canada, Russia and Norway.

The Arctic Ocean is in the Northern Hemisphere.

The deepest part of the Arctic Ocean is over **5 km deep.**

The Arctic Ocean is estimated to be **1.5 times** as big as the U.S.A.

The Arctic Ocean is extremely cold and has large icebergs floating on top of the water. During the winter, much of the ocean is covered by sea ice.

Animals such as walruses and whales live in the Arctic Ocean.

The Antarctic Ocean is the fourth largest ocean in the world. It is found in the Southern Hemisphere.

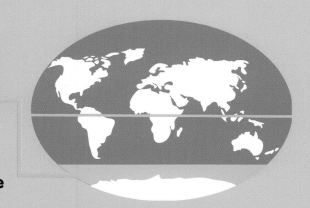

The Antarctic Ocean surrounds Antarctica. It is also known as the Southern Ocean because it is so close to the South Pole.

Scientists believe that the Antarctic Ocean formed 30 million years ago, which makes it very young in comparison to the other oceans!

Animals such as emperor penguins, fur seals and whales live in the Antarctic Ocean.

The Antarctic Ocean covers around 4% of the Earth's surface.

Similar to the Arctic Ocean, the Antarctic Ocean has icebergs floating on the surface of the water all year round. For many months of the year, the temperature of the water does not rise above 0 °C.

The icebergs in the Arctic and Antarctic Ocean make it difficult for boats to sail across them and special ice-breaker ships are often needed.

Tectonic Plates

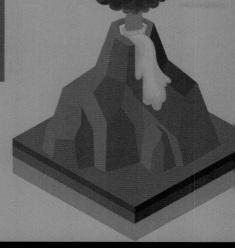

The Earth's outer layer is made up of solid rock. This rock is broken up into large pieces called tectonic plates.

Tectonic plates float on a layer of <u>molten rock</u> and are constantly moving. However, most of the time we cannot feel the tectonic plates moving.

Tectonic Plate Boundaries

— Tectonic plate

— Molten rock

Tectonic plates have been changing the face of the Earth for billions of years.

The Earth is covered by seven major plates and many other smaller plates.

The place where two different tectonic plates meet is called a plate boundary.

When tectonic plates push against each other, lots of different things can happen.

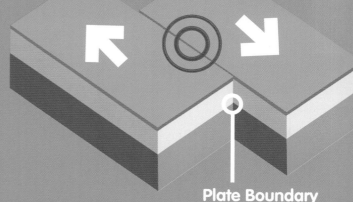

Plate Boundary

1) The plates may slide alongside each other. As the plates eventually slip past each other, the sudden jolt can cause an earthquake.

2) The plates may crash into each other, forcing one plate to slide underneath the other. This movement can cause molten rock to rise up between the plates, creating a volcano.

3) The plates may crash into each other, forcing one plate on top of the other. This can cause the ground to slowly rise up and eventually form mountains.

Tectonic plates can also move away from each other. As this happens, more molten rock rushes to the surface and, as it cools, it turns into rock.

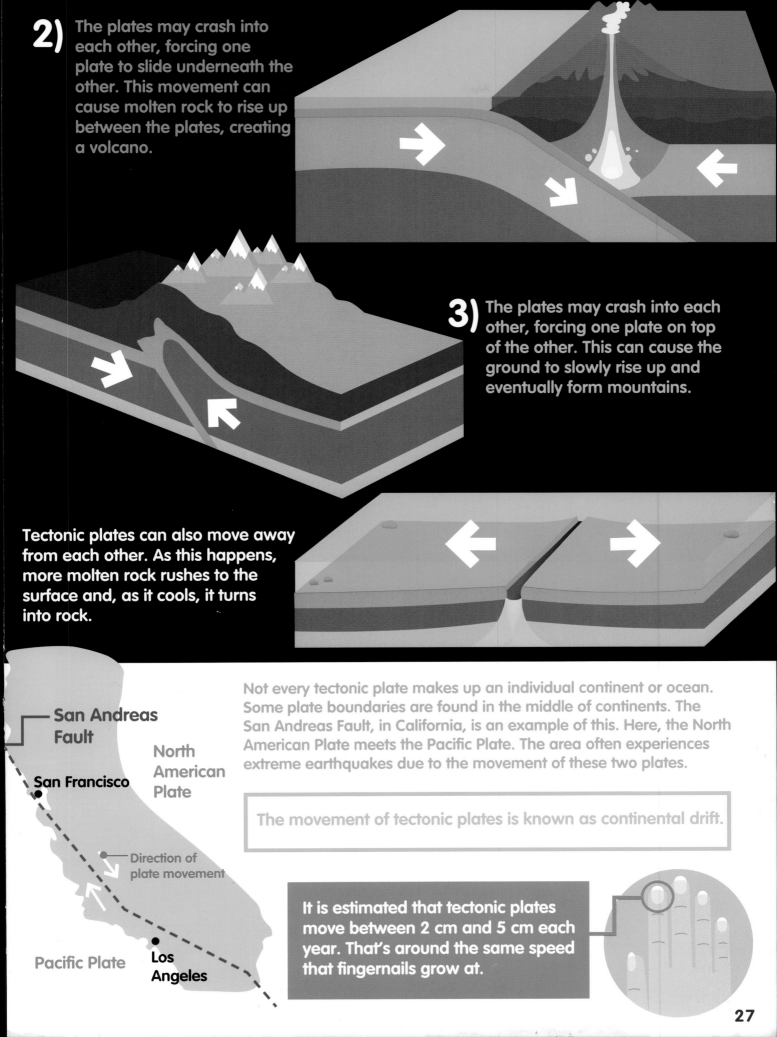

San Andreas Fault

North American Plate

San Francisco

Direction of plate movement

Pacific Plate

Los Angeles

Not every tectonic plate makes up an individual continent or ocean. Some plate boundaries are found in the middle of continents. The San Andreas Fault, in California, is an example of this. Here, the North American Plate meets the Pacific Plate. The area often experiences extreme earthquakes due to the movement of these two plates.

The movement of tectonic plates is known as continental drift.

It is estimated that tectonic plates move between 2 cm and 5 cm each year. That's around the same speed that fingernails grow at.

Continents Through Time

It is thought that over the course of history, the surface of Earth has changed. Over time, tectonic plates have moved, joined together and broken apart.

The first <u>supercontinent</u> was known as Rodinia. It is estimated to have formed **1.1** billion years ago!

Around **250** million years ago, **many landmasses joined together to form a huge supercontinent, known as Pangea.**

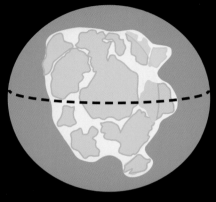

RODINIA

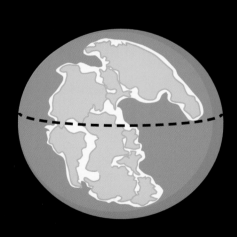

PANGEA

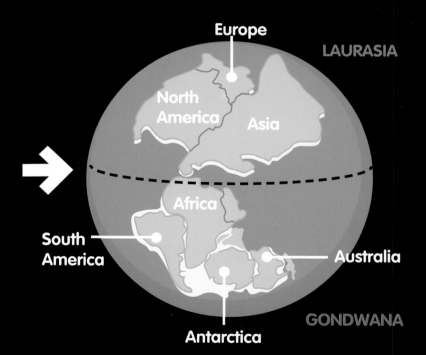

Europe

LAURASIA

North America

Asia

Africa

South America

Australia

Antarctica

GONDWANA

By around 150 million years ago, Pangea had separated into northern and southern landmasses. The northern part is known as Laurasia and the southern part is known as Gondwana. Laurasia eventually became North America, Europe and Asia. Gondwana broke up and became South America, Africa, Australia and Antarctica.

African Plate

Arabian Plate

Red Sea

In the Future ...

The Red Sea formed where the African and Arabian plates pulled apart. If they continue to drift apart, the Red Sea will eventually become an ocean.

All the tectonic plates will continue to move and drift as time passes until eventually, in another **one billion years** or so, the world could look totally different from how it does now!

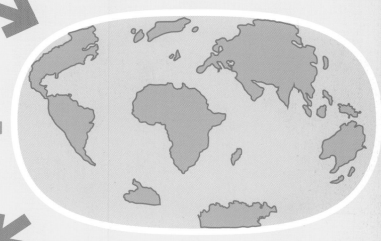

PANGEA PROXIMA

The world as we know it today will not last forever. In the future, the continents could move back together and form a **new version** of Pangea.

Activity

1 Copy this image onto a piece of paper as closely as you can.

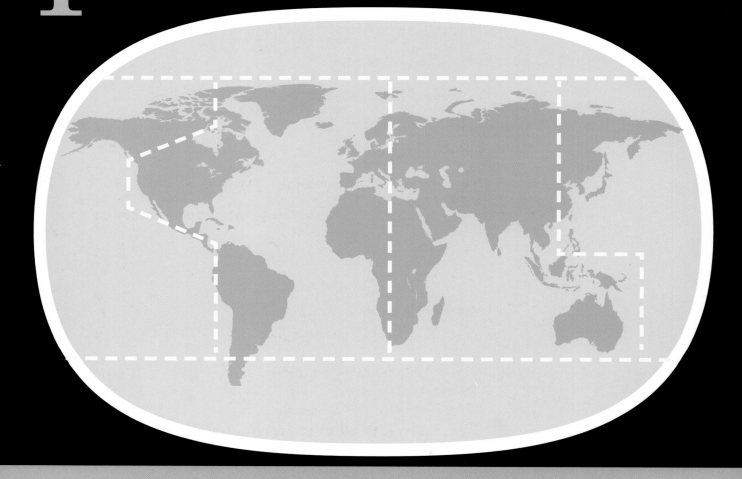

2 Label as many different **continents** as you can.

3 Label as many different **oceans** as you can.

Glossary

border	a line separating two countries
coral reef	a ridge of rock in the sea formed by the growth of coral
deserts	areas of land that receive very little rainfall
endangered	when a species of animal is in danger of becoming extinct
Equator	the imaginary line around the Earth that is an equal distance from the North and South Pole
glaciers	large masses of ice that move very slowly
hemispheres	halves of the Earth, usually divided by the Equator or the prime meridian
landlocked	almost or entirely surrounded by land
landmass	a continent or other large body of land
molten rock	rock that has been heated to such a high temperature that it has become liquid
oil	a type of fuel that formed over millions of years from the remains of plants and animals
phytoplankton	plankton made of very small plants
population	the number of people living in a place
prime meridian	the zero point of longitude
Richter scale	a numerical scale for showing the strength of an earthquake
savannahs	large areas of dry land with few trees and little grass
shallowest	the least deep
species	a group of very similar animals or plants that are capable of producing young together
summit	the highest point of a mountain
supercontinent	a cluster of several large landmasses that divided to create the continents we have today
surface	the outermost part of something
taigas	forest areas that often have swamps
uninhabited	not lived in

Index

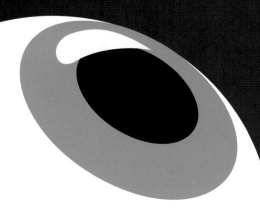